MISSION ME

The Journal

Printed in Canada
ISBN: 978-1-7361564-0-7
Second Edition

GoZen.com

☆ YOUR MISSION ☆

mission [mish-uhn]: an important task or duty, assigned or self-imposed; a goal that is accompanied by strong conviction.

Your mission, should you choose to accept it, is to use this journal to find the true you.

Work on the pages in order or jump around. Whatever you choose, one thing is mission critical: get this journal messy! Answer the questions, write in your thoughts, and please (no matter what age you are) don't skip the coloring quotes. :)

So, what do you say? Ready to dive in?

THIS MISSION WAS ACCEPTED BY:

Caroline Mary ♡

5-6-2⟩

Supersize your mission by listening
to the free KC podcast!

KC is the story of Kacey, a teen who loses
her memory right before her first day of high
school. With the help of friends, family, and the
mysterious KC, Kacey works to discover her true
self by using pages directly from this journal!

Listen here:

GoZen.com/podcast/

This journal is broken up into four missions.
Here they are!

MISSION #1:

Spot Your Strength Constellation

Everyone has hidden strengths. Learn how to spot
your greatest strengths, explore your passions,
and learn what makes you awesome.

MISSION #2:

Escape the Black Hole of Negative Thoughts

Discover the science of negative thoughts. Uncover how
they pull us in and what to do to escape their grip.

MISSION #3:

Ride Your Orbit of Feelings

Every feeling, no matter how cloudy or confusing, has a
source as well as an important message to deliver. Master
methods to feel your feelings and decode their messages.

MISSION #4:

Show Earth the Real You

Share the discovery of the real you with the rest of
the world. Learn to show up in any situation as the most
authentic, courageous, and confident version of yourself!

MISSION #1:

Spot Your Strength Constellation

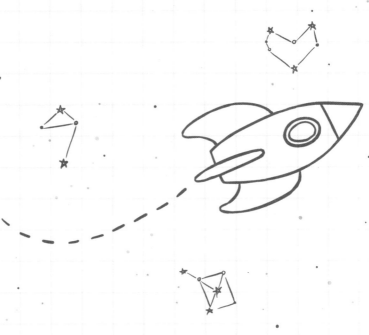

WHO AM I?

Without using your name, how would you finish
this sentence? I am <u>Cphfidint / bold / outspoken</u>.

Maybe you'd finish it with your sports skills: "I
am a soccer player." Maybe you'd lean on school
achievements: "I am a math whiz." Maybe you'd
talk about tough feelings: "I am such a worrier."

Here's the thing: interests and talents are
awesome, but they are only a small part of your
"me" story. Thoughts and feelings come and go
— they're temporary! The truth is, who you are
is far BIGGER than any experience, thought, or
feeling.

So... who are you? Who is your inner "me"?
We're about to find out. That's what this journal
is all about.

Mission #1 is to uncover a more permanent
part of your identity: your strengths. Are you a
leader? Are you funny? Are you loving? Once
you embrace your strengths, we're going to put
them to use and find an even bigger part of the
"me" puzzle: your purpose!

Sound intimidating? It's really not. Just have fun
and enjoy the exercises.

DON'T *YOU* EVER LET A

Soul IN THE World

~ TELL YOU ~

— THAT YOU CAN'T BE —

EXACTLY

WHO *YOU* ARE.

— Lady Gaga

THE SCIENCE IS CLEAR...

The Mission

55 scientists went on an adventure to figure out what's BEST about humans around the world.

The Research

These scientists read thousands of pages from books on philosophy, psychology, and youth studies: all from different cultures and different historical periods.

✦ YOU ARE STRONG! ✦

The Discovery

They figured out that while people around the world eat unique food, celebrate different holidays, and live in their own special way, they all have something in common: CHARACTER STRENGTHS.

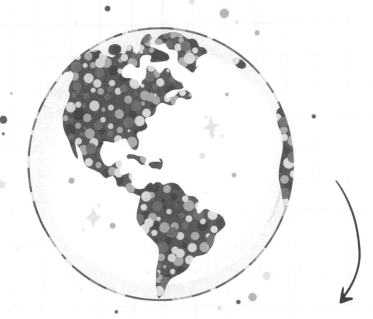

Great News!

Every human has 24 unique character strengths that show up in different amounts. These strengths help you overcome challenges, improve confidence, and become the most real version of you possible. It's time to uncover your strengths!

You're Awesome!

STRENGTH CONSTELLATIONS

Character strengths are the very best parts of you — your most positive qualities. Here are 24 strengths we all use in different amounts. Color in the ones you've used in your life:

Creativity Curiosity Judgment Love of Learning Perspective

Bravery Perseverance Honesty Zest

sometimes too much

Love Kindness Social Intelligence Teamwork Fairness Leadership

Forgiveness Humility Prudence Self Regulation

Appreciation of Beauty & Excellence Gratitude Hope Humor Spirituality

SPOT YOUR STRENGTHS

Check out the strengths in the sky above. Using the
key on the opposite page, put a circle around what you
think are your two greatest strengths. Put a square
around two strengths you'd love to work on.

STRENGTH SCAVENGER HUNT

Once you understand strengths, you start to see them all around you. Try this activity to uncover the strengths in your life.

If my three greatest strengths were made into songs, they would be called:

1. Stand out (Stand up)

2. In charge, take charge

3. I am Bold

The last time my friend needed help, I helped them by:

This is the strength I used:

If my greatest strength was a color, it would be: marble

Someone I look up to (a mentor, coach or teacher) shows these strengths:

5-6-21

This is a picture of someone I know with a strength I admire.

I use these strengths to get through challenging school assignments:

This is one of my favorite books:

_____.

These are the main character's greatest strengths:

I saw a complete stranger using this strength: perserverence.
This was awesome because: They were homeless but had 2 kids, 1 of which was a baby.

DESIGN YOUR OWN STRENGTHS SHIRT!

Show your awesomeness from the inside out by designing a shirt with your greatest strengths.

DESIGN YOUR OWN STRENGTHS KICKS!

Create your own celestial kicks! Maybe you want to
write or draw strengths you'd like to work on or maybe
the ones you admire most in other people. You can even
create your own strengths! No rules here. Just have fun!

WHAT WE KNOW MATTERS "but" WHO WE ARE MATTERS MORE.

— BRENÉ BROWN

WHAT WE KNOW MATTERS "but" WHO WE ARE MATTERS MORE?

— BRENÉ BROWN

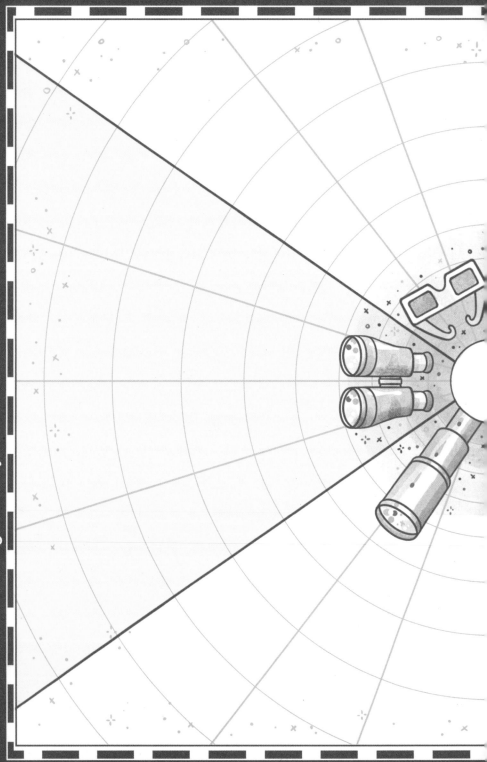

What strengths do you use when a friend needs advice?

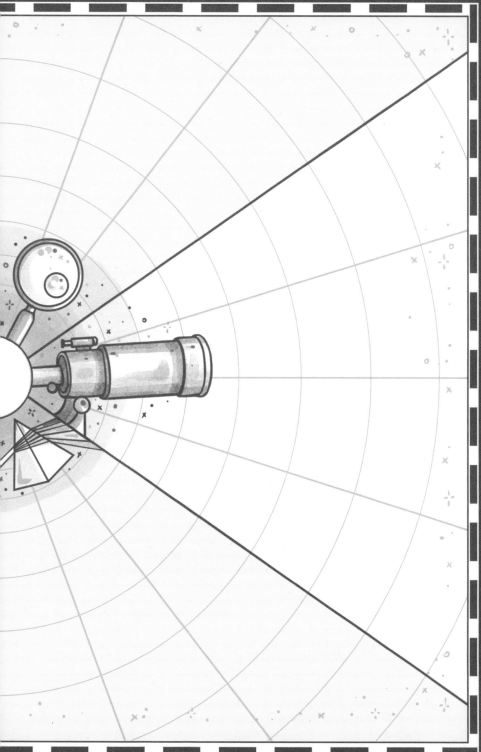

Imagine your best self 20 years from now. You've used all your strengths to create a meaningful, exciting life!

Now, pretend you're that future self and write a letter to the present version of you. Describe how you used your strengths to build an incredible life!

DEAR ME,

MY STRENGTHS STORY

DATE

MY STRENGTHS STORY

... LOVE, ME

TRACK YOUR STRENGTHS!

This is a strength tracker for one full month. Fill in the Tracker Key (bottom right of the opposite page) by writing one of your top strengths under each cirlce. Then, assign a color to each one.

For the next 31 days, fill in the color of the strength you used most during each day. Start with the star marked with a number one.

TRACKER KEY

WHAT LIGHTS YOUR FIRE?

What do you LOVE to do? Circle or color in some of your passions and interests below. Add in your own, too!

Painting/Drawing

Writing

Reading

Playing Music

Listening to Music

Cooking

Needlework

Photography

Hiking

Calligraphy

Singing

Dancing

Skating

Surfing/Paddling

DIY Projects

Gaming

Makeup

Gardening

Running/Jogging

Swimming

Biking

Martial Arts

26

WHAT DOES THE WORLD NEED?

You've probably been asked hundreds of times what you want to be when you grow up. What if someone asked you to think about what you'd like to contribute to the world? Fill the empty Earth below with the things you think the world needs most. Color it in for fun!

✶ FIND YOUR ICKY-GUY! ✶

In Okinawa, Japan, the average resident lives seven years longer than the average American. It's not uncommon for Okinawans to reach 100 years old! Researchers were interested in learning why.

In addition to differences in diet and relationships, the researchers discovered a difference in how Okinawans worked. They never retire — they don't even have a word for it! They do have a more interesting word: Ikigai.

Pronounced "icky guy," the word means "the reason you wake up in the morning." Think of it as your purpose — the reason you're excited about life. It's your driving force and your motivation!

WHAT'S YOUR IKIGAI?

Use the image below to help you find your Ikigai. List your passions, your strengths, and a few things the world needs. If you can discover ways that these three things intersect, you've discovered your Ikigai!

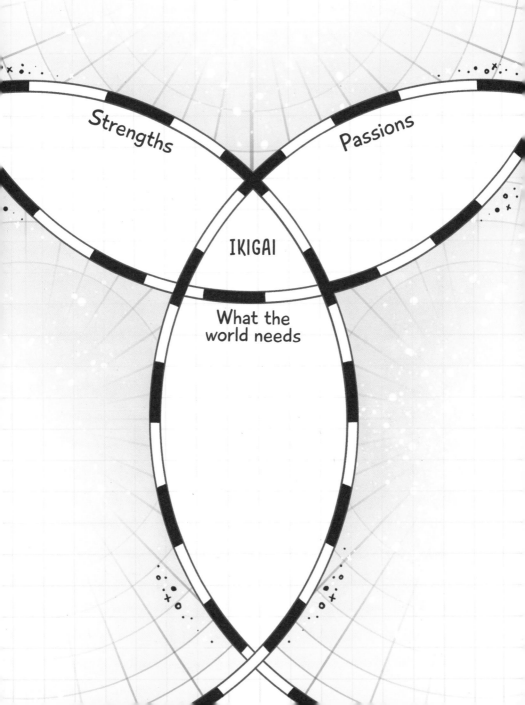

Strengths

Passions

IKIGAI

What the world needs

YOUR MIND

Some things

YOUR INNER VOICE,

YOUR INSTINCT,

KNOWS

Everything

-Henry Winkler

YOUR MIND

KNOWS ONLY

Some things

YOUR INNER VOICE,
YOUR INSTINCT,

KNOWS

Everything

—Henry Winkler

BE A TIME BENDER!

Have you ever played a sport, worked on art, or been so involved in an activity that it feels like time rushed by? Hours can feel like minutes when you're in "flow." Flow happens when the challenge of an activity is not so easy that you get bored AND not so hard that you get frustrated. When your skills are a perfect match for the challenge at hand, you find your flow!

What were you doing the last time you were in flow? How long were you actually doing the activity? How long did it feel like?

What character strengths did you use
the last time you were in flow?

MISSION #2:

Escape the Black Hole of Negative Thoughts

GOT THOUGHTS?

"I am going to fail."
"I am going to get laughed at."
"I am the worst at this."

We've all had negative thoughts. When they hit, they can be really hard to get rid of. They feel like the undeniable truth.

It's not enough for people to tell you these thoughts are not true. We know it's not enough for us to tell you that you have strengths and purpose — that you're amazing, and bright, and awesome — we know the most important thing is that you feel and believe those things yourself. You need to feel that your inner "me" is as perfect as you are.

And that's the tricky part, right? That's why you're here, on this mission. Feeling confident in who you are can be hard. Believe it or not, there are real scientific reasons why people focus on the bad parts of themselves. But don't worry... there are also real scientific things you can do about it.

It's time to start your next mission: seeing through the negativity.

THE GREATEST WEAPON

—AGAINST—

"STRESS"

IS OUR ABILITY TO

choose

ONE THOUGHT

OVER ANOTHER.

—William James

THE SCIENCE OF NEGATIVE THOUGHTS

What's right with this picture?

When it comes to people, situations in our lives, or even ourselves, it can be hard to focus on what's going right.

Blame your ancestors!

Think about cave people, the hunter-gatherers — true survivalists. The ones who thrived were aware of danger: the saber-toothed cat lurking in the bush; the storm clouds; the shifty glance from a neighbor. In other words, they were really paying attention to the bad stuff around them.

The Negativity Bias

While most of us aren't being chased by predators on our way to school, we still have what scientists call a Negativity Bias, where "bad stuff" attracts more of our attention than "good stuff."

Bad stuff still sticks

This is true even when it comes to how we view ourselves. The things we don't like about ourselves can really stick out like a sore thumb. However, some researchers thought it was time to help our brains start looking at the good.

·✦·✭ STICKY THOUGHT TESTER ·✭·✦·

Write some of your stickiest thoughts in the space below. What are some things that you find yourself thinking over and over again? Maybe they're thoughts about you. Maybe they're thoughts about school. Or maybe they're about life in general.

When you're done, use a red crayon to underline the negative thoughts and a green crayon for the positive thoughts. What kind of thoughts stick to you the most?

YOU CAN'T AVOID THOUGHTS

Negative thoughts make us uncomfortable, and they're hard to avoid. Most of the time, when people try to avoid negative thoughts, those thoughts just come back even stronger. You just can't shake them!

Try this: Put a timer on for 60 seconds and close your eyes. Before you start, make sure you don't think of a white bear. Ready? Go!

Was it hard? This is called the "White Bear Problem" or what happens when trying not to think about something actually makes you think about it even MORE!

✦ UNSTICK YOUR THOUGHTS ✦

Grab some sticky notes or just some scraps of paper and tape. Write some challenging thoughts on the sticky notes. Then, place them over the eyes below. Hard to see anything else, right? Now unstick them and move them further away from the eyes. The lesson: you don't have to get rid of challenging thoughts — just create a little space from them.

SPACE OUT YOUR THOUGHTS

Thoughts come and go. Sometimes thoughts are accurate, but many times they aren't true at all. You don't have to get rid of thoughts — just create some space between you and your thoughts.

✦ CREATE YOUR OWN SPACE ✦

Write some challenging or negative thoughts in the bubbles below. Draw yourself in the middle pushing those thoughts a little further away from you. Now, close your eyes and visualize these thoughts floating around you just like in the picture you've drawn.

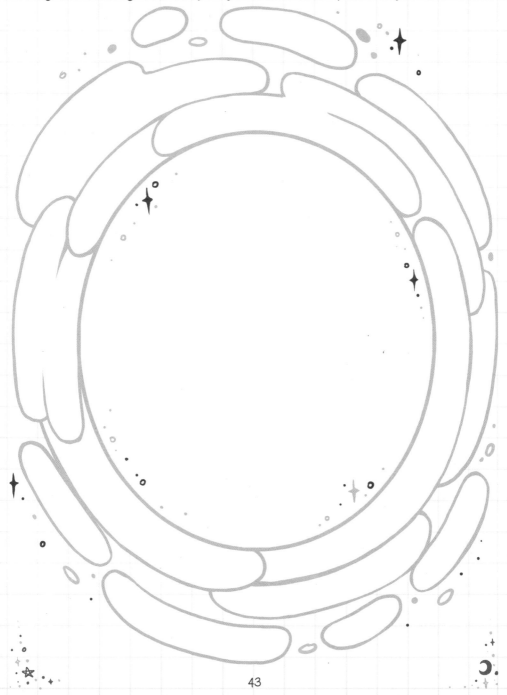

What if I
fail my math test?

I'm worried
I'll mess up at practice.

I feel like my friend
is mad at me.

I'm
stressed out.

I feel tired.

Science shows us that trying to get rid of, ignore, change, or run away from thoughts just makes them come back stronger. Instead, you can let your thoughts rise up and float by. They're still there, but you don't need to become one with your thoughts. Write some of your thoughts in the clouds and watch how they pass by.

44

✦ REPEAT AFTER ME: I AM ENOUGH ✦

Do you ever feel like you have to do more, be more, achieve more to just be enough?

Would you believe that you came into the world enough?

That's right. Without acing a class, winning a trophy, or impressing anyone on social media, you are enough.

In fact, you have always been enough, and you will always be enough.

Repeat this daily:

I am enough.
I am inspiring.
I am worthy.

I am authentic.
I am strong.
I am myself.

I am undefinable.
I am enough.

Use the space in the mirror to write your own positive affirmations or sayings. Fill in the sticky notes, fortune cookie slips, and even the mirror itself!

SELF-CONSCIOUSNESS IS THE ENEMY OF ALL ART, BE IT ACTING, WRITING, PAINTING, OR Living itself, WHICH IS THE GREATEST ART OF ALL.

-RAY BRADBURY

SELF-CONSCIOUSNESS IS THE ENEMY OF ALL ART, BE IT ACTING, WRITING, PAINTING, OR Living itself, WHICH IS THE GREATEST ART OF ALL.

- RAY BRADBURY

What if I mess up at practice, at practice, at praaaaactice, what if I mess up at practice, I guess it's not that big a deal!

I'm worried about my history test, my history teeeest, my history test! I'm worried about my history test, but I think I'll be OK!

Want to take some power away from those negative, sticky thoughts? Sing them to the tune of a nursery rhyme. Don't hold back — belt out your new song and watch humor melt away those thoughts!

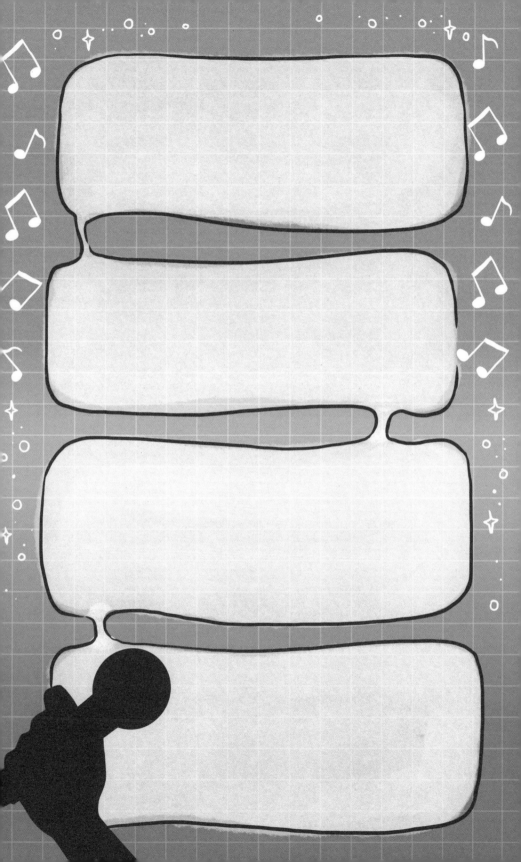

✦ "SHOULDS" SHOULD BE SHREDDED ✦

Goals are great, but if you think you "should" be something
or achieve something to feel like you're good enough
or even happy, then you need to SHRED that should.

SHRED SOME SHOULDS

In the ripped papers, write all the shoulds you want to shred!

NOTICE THOUGHTS FLOATING AWAY

Thoughts are just that: thoughts.
Sometimes thoughts are exaggerated or
inaccurate. Can you think of some thoughts
you've had that aren't really true?

Write your inaccurate thoughts
on the lanterns below and
watch them float away!

ON SECOND THOUGHT...

Ever worry and then worry about the fact that you worry?! You might have a first thought and then a second thought that judges the first thought.

In the example below, you'll see the first thought ("I'm so worried") and then a judgment or second thought about that first thought ("I hate that I'm thinking about being worried again"). Write some of your own first and second thoughts in the bubbles below.

SHIFT THE SECONDS

While you might not be able to change some first thoughts that pop into your mind, you can shift your second thoughts to OBSERVE instead of judge. Write out some first thoughts and then start your second thoughts with: "I notice I'm having the thought that..." Follow the example below.

I notice I'm having the thought that I'm so worried.

I'm so worried!

MISSION #3:

Ride Your Orbit
of Feelings

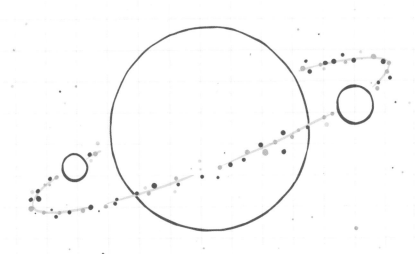

BIG FEELINGS!!!

"Stop getting so angry!"
"Don't cry all the time!"
"Go somewhere and calm down!"

Since early childhood, the message has been pretty clear: make your big feelings go away. And if you do have them, you better hide them or disappear until they're gone. Big bad feelings make other people uncomfortable.

Here's the thing: every human has those feelings, and every feeling you have, whether big or small, pleasant or uncomfortable, is only a message. If we hide our feelings, we'll never get the message, and we'll just keep having the same feelings over and over. Feelings are trying to tell you something about your inner "me," but they are NOT part of who you are.

It's time for your third mission. Let's learn how to read these messages, transform our feelings in a healthy way, and get comfortable with the fact that emotions are a big part of the experience of being you.

These Pains
— you feel are —
MESSENGERS.
⁂ Listen to THEM. ⁂

—Rumi

FEELINGS ABOUT FEELINGS

In the same way that we may have negative thoughts about our own thoughts, we can also experience bad feelings about our big feelings.

"Ugh, I feel really upset that I feel so angry all the time."

"I'm so scared and feeling scared makes me feel like a huge wimp."

"It's really depressing that I feel so sad."

The spaces inside the head on the opposite page represent different challenging emotions. Decide what emotion each space represents for you, and then write a few feelings you have about that feeling.

✦ FEELINGS FORTRESS ✦

Sometimes when we have an uncomfortable feeling, we build what we call a Feelings Fortress so we don't have to feel that feeling. The things we use to distract ourselves (e.g., TV, eating, social media) are the bricks, and they shut out more than just uncomfortable feelings.

What feelings do you think are being felt in the scene below? Write in the different feelings around the people below.

When you have feelings that make you uncomfortable, what do you usually do? Do you sit and feel your feelings, or do you try to distract yourself? Below are some examples of commonly used bricks. Circle the ones you use in your Feelings Fortress.

☆ Sleep

☆ Eat

☆ Work Out

☆ Watch TV

☆ Listen to Music

☆ Surf the Internet

☆ Stay Quiet

☆ Other (next page)

☆ BUILDING THE WALL BRICK BY BRICK ☆

When we build a Feelings Fortress, there's not a lot that can get through. Sure, it might give you temporary relief from your uncomfortable feelings, but you're also blocking new experiences, opportunities to find happiness, chances to make friends, or love from others. Fill in the bricks with your feelings blockers. On the right, write about the good things those blockers might prevent.

☆ ....
....
....
☆ ....
....
....
☆ ....
....
....
☆ ....
....
....
☆ ....
....
....
☆ ....
....

CHECK YOUR EMOTIONS' MESSAGES

Just because your emotions can't talk doesn't mean they have nothing to say. Emotions are always sending you messages, and they really need you to listen.

Me: Hey, Anger! I'm really feeling you right now. What's going on?

Anger:

Yeah, well your boundaries are being violated right now. You need to protect yourself!

Me: Hey, Worry! You're all I can hear in my head.

Worry:

Obviously! You have a huge math test in three days! You need a study plan!

Me: Guilt, why are you so intense right now?

Guilt:

It's about time you responded to me. I've been trying to tell you that what you said to your friend yesterday wasn't very nice.

✦ TALKING TO YOUR EMOTIONS ✦

Check out this list of emotions. Check the box next to
the emotion you'd like to have a conversation with.

☐ Anger   ☐ Guilt   ☐ Negativity   ☐ Envy

☐ Sadness   ☐ Worry   ☐ Other: _____

Now think about what this emotion looks like. Is it a person?
An animal? A fantastical character? What does their hair
look like? Is there a color you associate with the emotion? Do
they have any cool accessories? Draw your emotion below.

In the circle, draw the character you designed and write their name below. Now, create a conversation between you and your emotion.

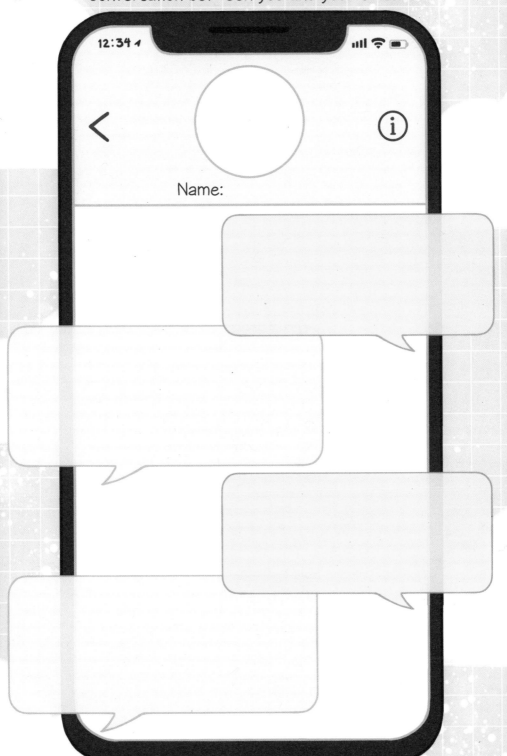

Name:

✴ FEELINGS FINDER ✴

What are you feeling right now? Circle your current feeling on the finder below. Write in more feelings you feel.

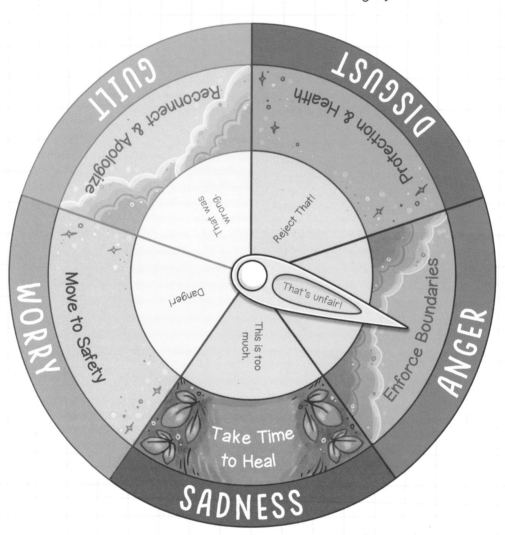

What message is your feeling sending?

✦ FEELINGS FINDER ✦

One of the best ways to recognize what you're feeling is by describing it. Use different colors to fill in the boxes below. Use the shade you think best describes each emotion.

ANGER	SADNESS	LOVE
DISGUST	JOY	WORRY
GUILT	EXCITEMENT	PRIDE

Using those colors, fill in the illustrations below with the location in your body where you feel three different emotions.

EMOTION: ....

Head / Face   Heart / Chest   Arms / Hands   Legs / Feet   Body / Stomach

EMOTION: ....

Head / Face   Heart / Chest   Arms / Hands   Legs / Feet   Body / Stomach

EMOTION: ....

Head / Face   Heart / Chest   Arms / Hands   Legs / Feet   Body / Stomach

THE FULL MESSAGE

Sometimes the things we say and do are only part of our emotional story. The same is true when we consider others' words and actions. There are the parts we see, and then there's the rest of the story.

✦ THE FULL MESSAGE ✦

Think of a time when you did or said something that was fueled by anger. What did others see or hear? Write it in the red section. What were the other pieces of the story? Surround your words with the rest of the story.

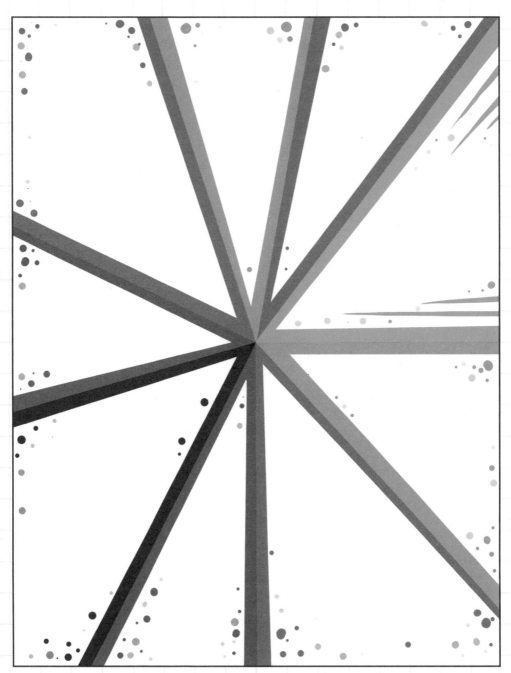

EVER FEEL LIKE A JELLYFISH?

Ever feel like people can see through you? Like they can see your emotions or thoughts? You're not alone. Researchers call this the Illusion of Transparency. We like to call it the Jellyfish Effect. Put a check next to the things you worry others can see. Then draw a picture of yourself as a see-through jellyfish.

☐ Blushing

☐ Shaky Voice

☐ Sweating

☐ Dizziness

☐ Soft Talking

☐ Loud Talking

☐ Fidgeting

☐ Not Making Eye Contact

☐ Nervous Laughing

☐ Write Your Own Below

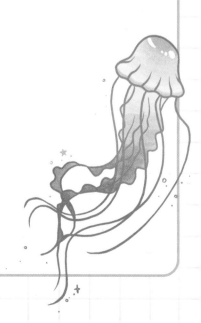

✦ ILLUSION OF TRANSPARENCY ✦

The Illusion of Transparency is just that: an illusion that others can hear your thoughts and feelings. Think of a time when you were really nervous. What did you think others saw? Now collect evidence by asking close friends what they really saw. What did you learn?

GIVING A SPEECH

What you think they see	What they actually see
Sweaty	
Nervous	
Shaky	

TALKING IN A GROUP

What you think they see	What they actually see
Your Nervous Thoughts	
Feeling Weird	
Uncomfortable	

What you think they see	What they actually see

Now, using your own thoughts, feelings, and evidence, draw what you think people see versus what they actually see.

These feelings can't hurt me

I can handle this experience

It's uncomfortable but not dangerous

This too shall pass

I'm Safe

MANTRAS TO MANAGE STRESS

Mantras are words or beliefs you can repeat to yourself. When you feel anxious, your body might feel uncomfortable, but you're safe. Repeating the mantra, "I'm uncomfortable, but safe" during really stressful times can help. Color in the image below and write in your own mantras.

MISSION #4:

Show Earth the Real You

I AM ME!

In Mission #1, you learned about who you really are. You discovered your strengths, your passions, and your purpose.

In Mission #2, you learned about the bad things we often think about ourselves, and how we can look past those to find the truth.

In Mission #3, we talked about how you are NOT your feelings, but that feelings can send you messages about what's important to you.

It's time now for your final mission. You're going to put what you've learned into action with a lot of different exercises. It's time to step into the world and show everyone who you are. You're going to find your courage and authenticity. You're going to discover who your people are, and where you really belong.

And most importantly, you're going to find the answer to the question we asked at the very beginning of this journal. When asked who you are, your best response is to say "I am ME." With no apologies.

BECAUSE true belonging ONLY HAPPENS WHEN WE PRESENT OUR AUTHENTIC, IMPERFECT, SELVES TO THE WORLD, OUR sense of belonging CAN NEVER BE GREATER THAN OUR LEVEL OF Self - acceptance.

-BRENÉ BROWN

CHOOSE YOUR OWN ADVENTURE!

Ever read a "Choose Your Own Adventure" story? You actually get to decide what the characters do. Your life is the ultimate CYOA story. When you have a decision to make, think about each choice and its potential outcome. Here's an example:

Hey! Wanna hang? The whole gang is here :)

"Do I go out with them? I don't know them that well. Maybe I'd be more comfortable at home. But it was nice of them to invite me. What if I go and it goes poorly? What if I don't go and I miss out on something awesome? I don't know what to do."

ADVENTURE #1 ✯

I could stay home and do nothing...   but then boredom and FOMO.

ADVENTURE #2 ✯

I could go out, but keep to myself and leave early...   but I might end up feeling awkward and silly.

ADVENTURE #3 ✯

I could go out and make an honest effort to talk and laugh...   which could result in a pretty good time.

✦ CHOOSE YOUR OWN ADVENTURE! ✦

Think about a dilemma you're facing. There's likely more than one course of action you can take. Think carefully about your options and their potential outcomes.

DILEMMA:

ADVENTURE #1 ✦

ADVENTURE #2 ✦

ADVENTURE #3 ✦

☆ ZONES ☆

In what zone do you spend the most time?
Circle the zone that feels most familiar to you.

Zone of Comfort

Our Comfort Zone is the space where you feel the most at ease. You don't have to meet new people, do new things, take risks, or do anything else we find uncomfortable, yet what you won't find inside our Comfort Zone is GROWTH.

Zone of Growth

In order to grow, you need to step into what we call our Zone of Growth, which is where you do the things that might at first seem a little uncomfortable but eventually help you grow stronger and more confident.

Zone of Distress

The Zone of Distress is a place where your tasks are so far above your current level of comfort that taking them on causes stress and confusion rather than growth.

On the next page, draw a picture of yourself in the middle of the zones. Next, fill in activities you do often, placing each one in the appropriate zone.

How can you make adjustments to be sure you spend the more time in the Zone of Growth? Remember, eventually things in the Zone of Growth will fall into your Comfort Zone and you can take on new challenges.

GET IN THE ZONE (EXAMPLE)

ZONE OF
GROWTH

ZONE OF
COMFORT

ZONE OF
DISTRESS

Giving a Speech

Telling a Friend
They Hurt
My Feelings

Making Eye Contact

No New People

No Risks

Trying Something New

Staying Home

Hanging with Siblings

Starting a Conversation

Dancing or Performing in Public

Speaking to Someone New

Reading in My Room

Cooking with My Mom

Asking Someone to Hang Out

Going Somewhere New by Myself

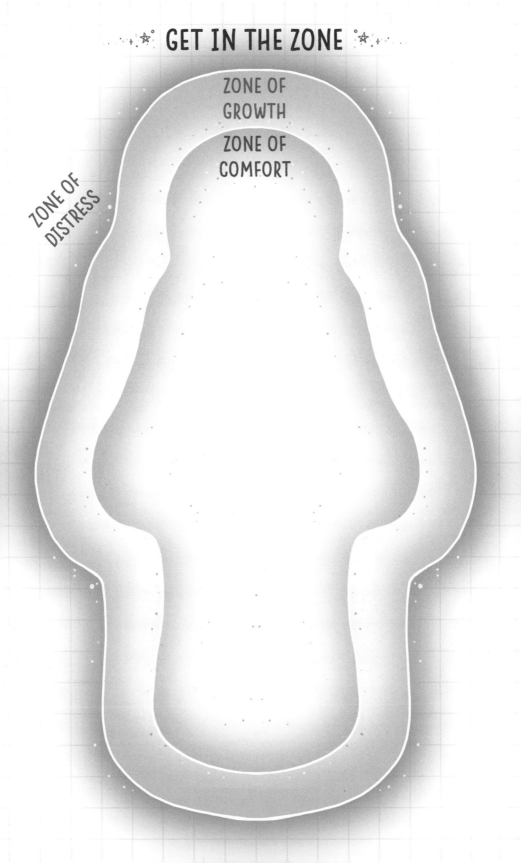

RACE TO REJECTION!

Things that are difficult get easier with practice; being rejected is no exception. While rejection hurts and most of us fear it, the more it happens, the easier it gets. You can practice getting rejected (really!) with this fun game.

The game: ask people for ridiculous stuff knowing full well that they're not only going to reject you, but they may even say you've lost it. Play with a friend. The player that racks up the most rejections/points wins the game!

Ask someone if you can borrow an obnoxious amount of money!

Suggest switching shoes with someone for the day!

Ask the lunch person to make you a steak instead of school lunch!

Add your own:

RACE TO REJECTION!

Go ahead and try your own Race to Rejection
using the guidelines below!*

10 PTS	20 PTS	20 PTS	50 PTS	50 PTS
PARENTS	SIBLINGS	FRIENDS	CLASSMATES	SCHOOL STAFF

Come up with your own Rejection Ideas and
check them off once you've done them!

10 PTS
20 PTS
50 PTS

10 PTS
20 PTS
50 PTS

10 PTS
20 PTS
50 PTS

TOTAL POINTS: _____

*Do this with the supervision of a grown-up; do not try
in unsafe conditions or with total strangers.

SURGE OF COURAGE

Ever seen a superhero movie? Did you notice that when superheroes use their powers, it's always in short bursts? You don't see them beaming lasers from their fingertips constantly. Believe it or not, the same goes for a hero's courage. In a crisis, the hero only needs to be brave for short bursts of time. We call this a Surge of Courage, and you can use this technique too!

Imagine if superheroes could carry their Surge of Courage around in a bottle and use it when they needed it the most, like an energy drink. What would it look like? Would it be a storm of lightning, a burst of stars, or bright hot flames? Try to imagine your own courage and create it in the bottle above!

USING YOUR SURGE OF COURAGE

What is it you want to do but haven't felt brave enough to try? Maybe it's as simple as making eye contact with someone, or as interactive as reaching out to a new friend.

Choose your mission, decide how long it will take, consume your bottled courage, and let's get it done!

Step 1: Choose your mission

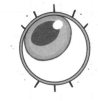

Make Eye Contact

Say Hi

Ask Someone to Hang Out

MY MISSION:

Step 2: Length of Time

☐ 10 Seconds   ☐ 30 Seconds   ☐ 60 Seconds

MY TIME:

Step 3: Go Do It!

☐ I DID IT!

COURAGE
DOESN'T MEAN YOU
don't get AFRAID.
COURAGE
means you
DON'T LET FEAR
STOP YOU.
~ Bethany Hamilton ~

COURAGE

DOESN'T MEAN YOU

don't get AFRAID.

COURAGE

means you

DON'T LET FEAR

STOP YOU.

~ Bethany Hamilton ~

COURAGE TRACKERS

Track your courage for two months! Color in the key on the next page using colors that represent bravery (or a lack of). Then color in one bottle each day to represent how brave you were.

COURAGE TRACKERS

Super
brave

Not so
brave

·∗· REFRAMING YOUR FEAR ∗·

When you have to perform (take a test, give a speech, etc.) sometimes your body does things that might not feel so good. Maybe your heart pounds or you sweat. Believe it or not, your body does those things to help you. If you reframe your nerves as excitement and acknowledge what your body is doing to help, it can change your entire experience for the better. Try it!

TUNNEL VISION ∗·

Nervous: I'm so nervous, I feel like I can't see straight!

Excited: I'm so excited, my body is hyperfocused so I don't mess up!

HEART RACING ∗·

Nervous: I'm so nervous, my heart is beating so fast it's scaring me!

Excited: I'm so excited, I feel like I could run a marathon!

DIZZINESS ∗·

Nervous: I'm so nervous, my thoughts are going round and round!

Excited:

SWEATING ∗·

Nervous: I'm so nervous, my hands won't stop sweating!

Excited:

SHAKING ∗·

Nervous: I'm so nervous, I can feel my whole body shaking!

Excited:

⋆ YOUR BODY CAN TAKE IT! ⋆

Nervousness and excitement can be two sides of the same card — your body feels almost the same in both. Read the word on the card and write out some situations where that feeling actually means you're excited and not scared!

I'M EXCITED!

I'M EXCITED!

Right before riding a rollercoaster!

When I'm watching a horror movie!

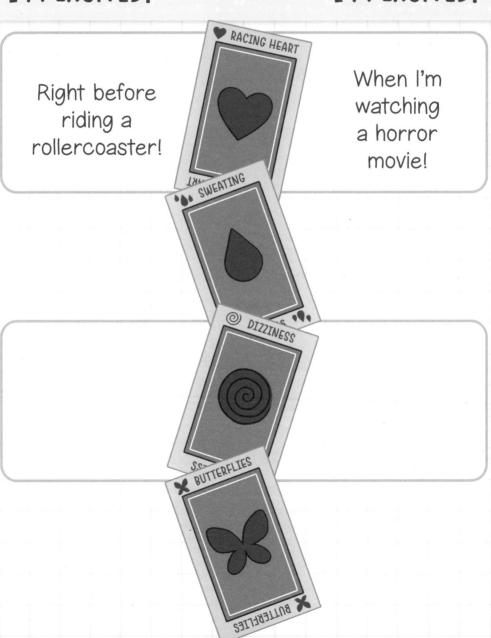

F-E-A-R

HAS TWO MEANINGS:

"FORGET EVERY- THING AND RUN"

OR

"FACE EVERY- THING AND RISE"

THE CHOICE IS YOURS.

-ZIG ZIGLAR

WHEN YOU SAY WHAT YOU DON'T MEAN

It shouldn't be a challenge to say what's in our heads or in our hearts. But when faced with "popular" opinions, we often find ourselves silencing our own voices. What are we afraid of? Looking like we're not cool? Getting into an argument?

Write a few reasons why you've kept your inner voice quiet during situations like this.

☆ OWNING YOUR OWN OPINION ☆

When your opinion isn't popular, you might feel like you want to change it in order to fit in. In the lightning bolts, write in some of the things you're feeling when you go against a popular opinion.

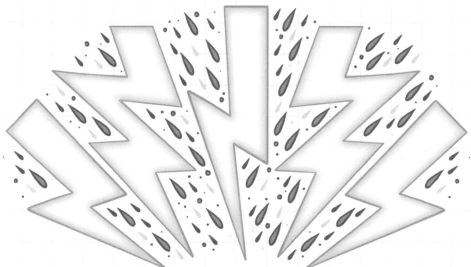

In the tree roots below, write in a few words or phrases that you feel best express the reasons why you stick behind some of your own opinions. These could be your strengths. Even if you have to stand alone, it's OK to be rooted in your own opinions if that is what feels right, no matter what anyone else says.

HOW YOU STAY STRONG IN A STORM

TRY AGAIN, AS YOUR AUTHENTIC SELF

In the long run, do you think this interaction will go better or worse than the last example? What do you think some of the responses will be? If they're not positive responses, how can you handle it?

TWO ROADS
diverGed
IN A WOOD,
AND I-I
took the
ONE LESS
TRAVELED BY,
And that
HAS MADE
ALL the
DIFFER ENCE.
-Robert Frost

TWO ROADS
diverGed
IN A WOOD,
AND I-I
took the
ONE LESS
TRAVELED BY,
And that
HAS MADE
ALL the
DIFFER ENCE.
-Robert Frost

⋆ TRANSFORMING JUDGMENT...⋆

Below you see one person jumping to the wrong conclusion about what the other is thinking. Sometimes, if you think you're being judged, it may just be a reflection of your own self-doubt.

... INTO CURIOSITY

What would this scene look like if both people have more curiosity instead of feeling judged or being judgmental? Write in possible curious thoughts below.

HEART & HEAD MISALIGNMENT

Have you ever felt conflicted about a decision you needed to make? Maybe your thoughts were saying one thing, but your feelings were saying another. When you have a difficult choice ahead of you, it's helpful to weigh ALL the information.

HEART & HEAD MISALIGNMENT

Think of a difficult decision you have had to make or have coming up. Using the scales, write the messages from your head on the left and the messages from your heart on the right. Which side do you usually listen to?

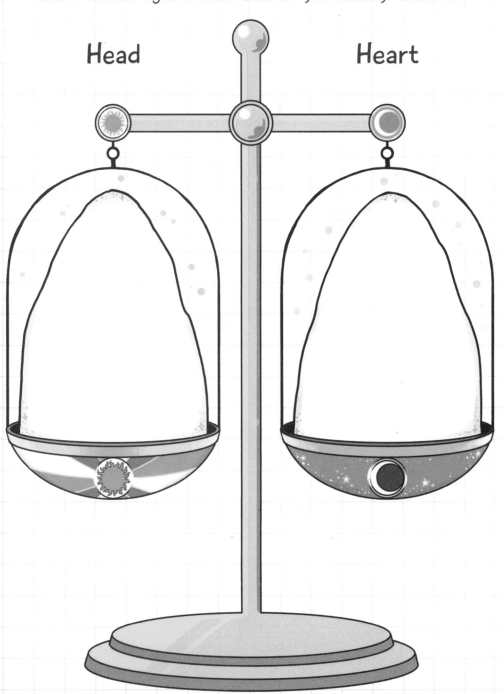

Head

Heart

SOCIAL SKILLS FAUX PAS!

We all make these social errors at times. Circle some that you've done in the recent past:

Eye Contact

Look Down
You don't want to miss out on the world's most interesting speck of dirt!

Just Close Them
Don't look. Seriously, you're better off not looking!

100% Staring
Unblinking. Never look away, not even for a second.

Handshake

CRUSH HAND!!!
The stronger the handshake, THE MORE CONFIDENT!

Slap It Away
Like, ew. Germs.

Give One Finger
It'd be hilarious. Nothing breaks the ice like a good laugh!

Posture

Absolute Stillness
So stiff, so rigid: like a board!

Puff Out Your Chest!!!
Extra points for the superhero shirt bust!

Folded Arm Slouch
Bonus? Top this one off with a scowl.

✷ SOCIAL SKILLS SUPERPOWERS ✷

What do you want to try improving? Color in
the area you're going to work on below!

Eye Contact

60-70% Eye Contact

Researchers found that
the ideal amount of eye
contact was 60-70%. Eye
contact means making
a connection. Having a
hard time? Try to notice
the person's eye color
during a conversation.

Handshake

Like a Peach

When checking a fruit
for ripeness, you squeeze
just hard enough to
check for resistance,
but not so hard that
your bruise it. The same
rule applies for people!

Posture

"Here I Am" Pose

Chest forward, shoulders
back and down, chin
and forehead aimed
forward or slightly up.
Allow yourself to take
up space and be at
ease in that space. You
deserve to be here!

THE BRAIN ON BELONGING

Has anyone ever told you that all you need is one good friend?
Turns out, this is backed by science. Research shows that
one good connection can boost your sense of belonging. What
situations make you feel completely comfortable, like you belong?
Write some in below and draw some on the opposite page!

FEELING BELONGING

Practicing my favorite hobby	Listening to my favorite music

Singing in the shower	Being surrounded by my family

IMHO, I feel like I belong most when I am:

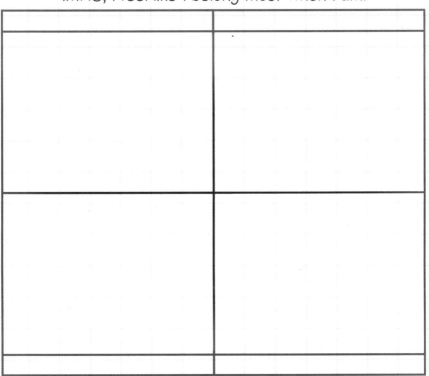

WHO ARE YOUR PEOPLE?

The people with whom you feel most like yourself are your team. Your peeps. Your posse. Together they connect and form a web around you, holding you up and supporting your true self. Not sure who your peeps are? Haven't formed your web yet? No problem! Use the prompts below to get you started, and use the web on the next page to start building your network. Draw faces, or just write names. Psst... it's OK if one person fills in more than one place, or if you can't think of anyone for a few of the prompts.

....

☆ This person makes me laugh until my stomach hurts:

☆ I'm most myself around this person:

☆ The person I miss the most when they're not around is:

☆ This is the person I go to for advice when I need it:

☆ This person makes me feel like I'm amazing just for being me:

⋅⋅✦ ARE YOU GOOD TO YOU? ✦⋅⋅

We tend to spend time worrying about the way we're treated by others. But how much time do we spend focused on the way we treat ourselves? Science shows there are three essential pieces to self-compassion. Next time you're starting to feel bad about something you did or said or just in general, practice the three components of self-compassion below:

1. FEEL THE FEELS

Say: "Difficult feelings are a part of life. I feel

_____

(feeling) and that's OK."

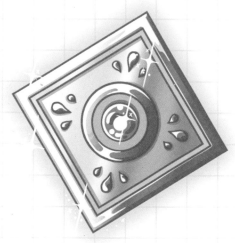

2. BE YOUR OWN BFF

Say: "If my best friend were here, they would say this about what I'm going through:

_____

_____"

3. CONNECTION

Say: "I'm not alone in how I feel. Everyone struggles and has challenges. It's just part of being human."

SELF-COMPASSION TRIFECTA

When joined together, the three components (officially known as mindfulness, self-kindness, and common humanity) make up the Trifecta of Self-Compassion! Once you have attained all three, connect the pieces together and get ready to take on the world! Draw yourself holding the trifecta high over your head!

FROM SELF-CRITICISM TO SELF-COMPASSION

Jade needs help practicing self-compassion. Cross out the words she is saying to herself and write in ones that are more self-compassionate.

The challenge: I screwed up and served the final point into the net.

Later that day:

I can't believe I screwed up at the match point.

Yeah, you lost the game for your team. Everyone must be upset!

Why did I do that? I should've practiced harder. UGH! I'm the worst teammate ever!

No one knows how this feels.

I'm alone in this.

It's easy for everyone else.

TALKING TO YOUR BFF

Check out these two conversations. What do they have in common? In what ways are they drastically different?

> I can't believe I didn't make the team. We practiced all summer for it. I feel like I shouldn't have even bothered x(

> Don't be so hard on yourself! I was your practice partner so I know how well you play. There were so many factors out of your control.

> Ya but I feel like everyone else was just so much better than me. I shouldn't have even tried.

> Listen, this wasn't the be-all end-all, and I'm sure nerves got in the way. You're a great player, don't stop trying! :)

> ... I guess you're right. I guess I can always try again :)

> Of course you can. If you don't I'll throw a basketball at you :P

> Hey! LOL, aren't you supposed to be my friend?

> Obviously, I meant PASS a basketball to you LOLOL

TALKING TO YOURSELF

Wow. I can't believe I didn't make the team. I practiced so hard, and it was like it didn't even matter. I feel like I shouldn't have even tried.

I mean really tho, why did you try? You know you're no good at this anyway. Your friend didn't even get in, and they're pretty good.

... I know but... ugh I just thought if I worked hard enough I'd be able to make the team! Was my hard work just not enough?

Of course it wasn't. You gotta account for talent too right? And let's be real, you didn't try hard enough.

... You're right. I could've tried so much harder.

And why do you think your BFF didn't make it?

Because I was a bad partner?

Exactly.

127

✦ TALKING TO YOUR BFF ✦

Your friend is having a really hard time. Imagine a conversation between the two of you. Talk to them like any good friend would. Be supportive, caring, and a good listener.

My teacher called my mom and told her I haven't been paying attention in class. My mom is really mad! It's not even true!

TALKING TO YOURSELF

Now it's you that's having the hard time. Your thoughts are pretty negative, and you need to help yourself get through it. Start the conversation with a challenge you're facing.

✦ LOVING-KINDNESS MEDITATION ✦

Scientists have proven that practicing loving-kindness meditation can make us more grateful, more joyful, and even more social! Try saying the words of this meditation to yourself:

May I be happy,
healthy, and peaceful.

May I let go of sadness
and bad feelings.

May I be free from anger.

May I be free from pain.

May I be free from difficulties.

May I be free from suffering.

May I be healthy, happy,
and peaceful.

May I be filled with
loving-kindness.

May I be at peace.

SPREADING THE LOVING-KINDNESS OUT

I spread this loving-kindness out.

I send love to my family, friends, the
earth, & all beings of the universe.

May they let go of sadness and bad feelings.

May they be free from anger.
May they be free from pain.

May they be free from difficulties.
May they be free from suffering.

May they be healthy, happy, and peaceful.

May they be filled with loving-kindness.

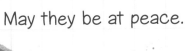

May they be at peace.

BEST FUTURE SELF

Picture your absolute Best Future Self. On the next page, draw your current self looking at your Best Future Self through the wormhole. Add items you think would help describe future interests. Then write down the details below your image!

Confident and Strong
Boxing & Martial Arts Enthusiast
Epic Fashion Sense
Successful, Hardworking
Well Traveled and Educated

BEST FUTURE SELF

WHEN YOU WISH

Trying to count the possibilities for yourself, your life, and your relationships is like trying to count the stars. On the opposite page, gaze into the night sky and write just a few of the things you wish for your future. Then, in the space below, draw a picture of yourself that includes as many of those wishes as you can fit coming true.

EXTRA GOOD STUFF!

On the following pages, you'll find descriptions of all 24 character strengths, followed by a list of references to the science behind this journal.

Check out GoZen.com for even more fun.

24 STRENGTHS AND WHAT THEY MEAN

WISDOM

These are brain strengths that cover learning new things, using your knowledge, and thinking hard to solve problems.

Creativity:

Having new ideas. Thinking of new ways to do things. Sure, these could be artistic creations, but they don't need to be. Maybe you're creative with science. Or words. Or even music.

Curiosity:

Trying new things just to try them. Finding new subjects and topics fascinating., including exploring and discovering.

Judgment:

Thinking things through from all sides. Being a patient and rational thinker. You're very fair and don't jump to conclusions. Plus, you're able to change your mind if you get new information.

Love of Learning:

Getting as much information as you can about topics you love. This can also involve mastering as many skills as you can. Sound like curiosity? It's related, but a Love of Learning means you keep adding, and adding, and adding to what you know.

Perspective:

Giving good advice to others. You have ways of looking at the world that make sense to yourself and to other people. This is similar to judgment, but involves less decision-making and is more about understanding the big picture.

24 STRENGTHS AND WHAT THEY MEAN

COURAGE

These are emotional strengths that involve using your willingness to accomplish challenging goals, no matter how hard they might be.

Bravery:

Not backing down from a threat, challenge, or difficulty. You do what is right even if others disagree and stick to your beliefs even if it makes you unpopular. Bravery can be physical or mental.

Perseverance:

Finishing what you start, even if there are obstacles. You get things done, and it makes you feel good.

Honesty:

Speaking the truth, always. You talk and act like you, and you don't try to be anything else. You take responsibility for your feelings and actions.

Zest:

Approaching life with excitement and energy. Nothing is half-hearted for you. Life is an adventure, and it makes you feel alive.

24 STRENGTHS AND WHAT THEY MEAN

HUMANITY

These are friendship strengths that involve being good to people: family, friends, anyone.

Love:

Valuing close relations with others, especially when your feelings are returned. You're good at being close to people.

Kindness:

Doing favors and good deeds for others. You like helping people and taking care of them.

Social Intelligence:

Being aware of the motives and feelings of other people and yourself. You know how to fit into different social situations, and show up the right way for the right people.

24 STRENGTHS AND WHAT THEY MEAN

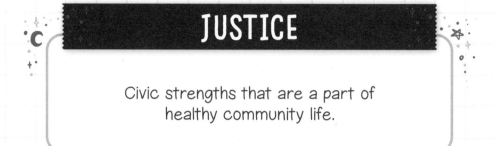

JUSTICE

Civic strengths that are a part of
healthy community life.

Teamwork:

Working well as a member of a group or team. You're loyal
to the group, and you always do your fair share.

Fairness:

Treating all people the same no matter who they are or
where they come from. You give everyone an equal chance.

Leadership:

Encouraging a group you're a part of to get things done. You
try to keep good relationships with everyone in the group.
You're good at organizing efforts and seeing that jobs get
finished.

24 STRENGTHS AND WHAT THEY MEAN

TEMPERANCE

Personal strengths that keep you and
your abilities in perspective.

Forgiveness:

Forgiving those who have done wrong. You accept the
shortcomings of others, and you're willing to give people
second (maybe even third) chances. Revenge is not a word
in your vocabulary.

Humility:

Letting your accomplishments speak for themselves. You
don't need to talk about yourself, or think about yourself, in
exaggerated ways.

Prudence:

Being careful about your choices, not taking unnecessary
risks. You don't say or do things that you'll regret.

Self-Regulation:

Controlling what you feel and do. You have great discipline
and control over your appetite and emotions.

TRANSCENDENCE

Appreciation strengths that create connections to the larger universe and give meaning to life.

Appreciation of Beauty and Excellence:

Noticing awesomeness in all things, including nature, art, math, science, and everyday life.

Gratitude:

Being aware of and thankful for the good things that happen. You take time to say thank-you.

Hope:

Expecting the best for the future and working to get there. Believing that a good future is something you can make happen.

Humor:

Liking to laugh and make others laugh. Your gift is bringing smiles to other people. You see the light side of things, make jokes, and generally spread happiness.

Spirituality:

Having beliefs about the higher purpose and meaning of life. You know where you fit in the world, and you have beliefs that shape what you do.

REFERENCES

Many of the exercises on your mission were inspired by some incredible science! Here are some references:

Brown, M. A., & Stopa, L. (2007). The spotlight effect and the illusion of transparency in social anxiety. *Journal of Anxiety Disorders, 21*(6), 804-819. doi:10.1016/j.janxdis.2006.11.006

Buettner, D. (2012). *The Blue Zones: 9 lessons for living longer from the people who've lived the longest.* Washington, D.C.: National Geographic.

Csikszentmihalyi, M. (2009). *Flow: The psychology of optimal experience.* New York: Harper Row.

Eisenberger, N. I., Lieberman, M. D., & Williams, K. D. (2004). Does rejection hurt? An fMRI study of social exclusion. *PsycEXTRA Dataset.* doi:10.1037/e633912013-635

Fredrickson, B. L., Cohn, M. A., Coffey, K. A., Pek, J., & Finkel, S. M. (2008). Open hearts build lives: Positive emotions, induced through loving-kindness meditation, build consequential personal resources. *Journal of Personality and Social Psychology, 95*(5), 1045-062. doi: 10.1037/a0013262

Harris, R. (2019). *Act made simple: an easy-to-read primer on acceptance and commitment therapy.* Oakland, CA: New Harbinger Publications, Inc.

Jamieson, J. P., Mendes, W. B., Blackstock, E., & Schmader, T. (2010). Turning the knots in your stomach into bows: Reappraising arousal improves performance on the GRE. *Journal of Experimental Social Psychology, 46*(1), 208-212. doi: 10.1016/j.jesp.2009.08.015

King, A. (2001). The health benefits of writing about life goals. *Personality and Social Psychology Bulletin, 27*(7), 798-807.

Meevissen, Y. M. C., Peters, M. L., & Alberts, H. J. E. M. (2011). Become more optimistic by imagining a best possible self: Effects of a two week intervention. Journal of *Behavior Therapy and Experimental Psychiatry, 42,* 371-378.

Neff, K. (2013). *Self compassion.* London: Hodder & Stoughton.

Peterson, C., & Seligman, M. E. P. (2004). *Character strengths and virtues: a handbook and classification.* New York: Oxford University Press.

See also viacharacter.org.

Warren, R., Smeets, E. & Neff, K. D. (2016). Self-criticism and self-compassion: Risk and resilience for psychopathology. *Current Psychiatry, 15*(12), 18-32.

Supersize your mission by listening
to the free KC podcast!

KC is the story of Kacey, a teen who loses
her memory right before her first day of high
school. With the help of friends, family, and the
mysterious KC, Kacey works to discover her true
self by using pages directly from this journal!

Listen here:

GoZen.com/podcast/